FINDING, ACCEPTING, AND LOVING
THE FATHER'S HEART!

In Search of the King's Court

A COMPILATION OF POWERFUL DEVOTIONS BY
CHARLANA KELLY

In Search of the King's Court
Finding, Accepting, and Loving the Father's Heart
Copyright © 2006 by Charlana Kelly

All rights reserved. No part of this book may be reproduced or transmitted in any form or by any means without written permission from the author.

> Unless otherwise noted, all Scripture is taken from the New King James Version. Copyright © 1982 by Thomas Nelson, Inc. Used by permission. All rights reserved." Scripture marked **AMP** "Scripture quotations taken from the Amplified® Bible Classic, Copyright © 1954, 1958, 1962, 1964, 1965, 1987 by The Lockman Foundation Used by permission." (www.Lockman.org) Scripture quotations marked **MSG** are taken from THE MESSAGE, copyright © 1993, 2002, 2018 by Eugene H. Peterson. Used by permission of NavPress, represented by Tyndale House Publishers. All rights reserved. Scripture marked **NIV** are taken from the Holy Bible, New International Version®, NIV®. Copyright © 1973, 1978, 1984 by International Bible Society. Used by permission of Zondervan Publishing House. All rights reserved. Scripture quotations marked **NLT** are taken from the Holy Bible, New Living Translation, copyright 1996. Used by permission of Tyndale House Publishers, Inc., Wheaton, Illinois 60189. All rights reserved.

Cover image:
Published by:

www.speaktruthmedia.com
PO Box 1448, Crockett TX 75835-7448

For information about special discounts available for bulk purchases, sales promotions, fundraising, and educational needs, contact by email: SpeakTruth Media Group LLC at order@speaktruthmedia.com.

ISBN 978-1-7364520-2-8 *(pb)*

First Edition Printed in USA 2006
Second Edition Printed in USA 2021

Dedication

To everyone who hungers for MORE, who resists surface dwelling and longs for the deep recesses of God in Heaven. To those who will not be denied the true riches of knowing Christ fully and intimately. This book and the words in it are dedicated to YOU, your life and your future in Him! They are a calling upward to your high call in Christ!

Contents

Foreword 8
Introduction 10
An Invitation to Greatness 26
Destiny Makes Demand 36
Times of Preparation 42
Walk in the Spirit 47
Being Led by the Spirit 54
Expressions of God 58
Benefits of Surrender 61
The Blessings of Doing 69
Guarding Your Gates 73
Eyes UP 78
Anxiety be Gone 81
No Fear Lives Here 89
Rhythms of Grace 93
Be it Unto Me 97
The Key of David 102
Living Selflessly 108
Hope of Glory 118
High Calling 131
Declare Him 135
Epilogue – Answer the One Who Calls 142

Foreword

Although God does not play favorites, and He is no respecter of persons, you still see people operating at and living at many different levels of life and ministry. There are several factors that determine these differences. Passion, compassion, faithfulness, initiative, faith, purity, hunger, and humility are just a few of these vital factors that make all the difference, even though we all start out on the same level playing field.

Then there are those extraordinary individuals who have not only discovered these vital factors and are using and growing in them, but they are committed, even driven to help others discover these life-changing keys.

The above is a precise description of Charlana Kelly.

It is my pleasure to have served as her pastor for more than a twenty years and to watch her grow, discover, rejoice, reach out, duplicate, give glory to God, and then grow some more. It is also my pleasure to recommend her and this writing to you as she expresses insights and accounts of God working in and through her life. As you read this book, you will be touched and helped to higher ground!

Tim Gilligan, Founding Pastor
Meadowbrook Church Ocala, Florida

Introduction

In Search of the King's Court

Have you ever felt like you are destined to do something more than you are doing today? Something life-changing? Something great? I have believed something extraordinary would happen in my life since childhood. It's been a mystery for most of my life, and now I feel like I have a clue of what this greatness might be in the days ahead.

I often felt like I should have lived in a different era or a foreign nation in my early years. As a small child, I remember asking God regularly why I was not born in a country where monarchy ruled. I was *certain* that I should have been born somewhere else because I should have been born a princess. It was my greatest desire! And being born in America, well, that did not hold any promise! My mother indulged her small child by enrolling me in ballet to teach me how to be graceful. My first recital? Of course, Cinderella! What more could I ask!?! I played the scenario over in my mind, dreaming of the royal court, longing even then for the court of a king!

MEETING THE ROYAL INFANT

God blessed me with two incredible parents, who adopted me as an infant. My mother, whose heritage in the Lord could be traced back generations, would sit me on the couch and read the Bible to me daily. Jesus was a name I was familiar with as a small child. I loved Him because I loved everyone, no matter who they were. I heard He was a gift given to me from God, though I did not know Jesus as Savior. I knew what I was hearing, but the words never made it to my heart. I heard that I should love Him and that He loved me, so with childlike faith, I just accepted it and loved Him even more.

One of my greatest treasures at four years old was a tiny baby Jesus in a walnut shell that I made at preschool. I carried the makeshift manger around for months, thinking it a priceless treasure entrusted to my care.

AN ENCOUNTER WITH THE KING

Jesus even visited me as a small child. He told me that He would return in my lifetime, which I promptly repeated to my mother. I'll never forget her response when I blurted it out from the back seat of our 1960s station wagon. She abruptly pulled the car off the road. Shocked, she began trying to convince me otherwise. From that moment forward, I believed what Jesus told me will come to pass. And *certainly*, to this day, I still believe He will come back in my lifetime, now more than ever.

READING THE KING'S LETTER

As I grew older, my mother no longer read the Bible to me; it was time for me to read it myself. She purchased me a copy of the 1970s The Way Bible, thinking the everyday language would help me understand it clearly. A voracious reader, I devoured that Bible from cover to cover. When I read Jesus' words to Nicodemus, "You must be born again," they touched my heart, bringing me to tears. I surrendered my life to the Lord then and there, alone in my bedroom at ten years old with no preacher, no evangelist, no one else, just me, my Savior, and my heavenly Father. God and His Son were now real to me.

PRAYING TO MY KING

Each night I prayed on my own about the poor, the needy, the lame, the sick, and the blind, because the words I read in the Bible said to do it, and I believed every word! "God heal them all and bless them," I would pray, often in tears. I remember those moments in my heart now. They were powerful times with the Lord. I knew His presence, and His Spirit was so strong in my life.

Jesus had hold of my heart, and He would never let it go, although I would eventually let go of Him.

ENTICED AWAY FROM MY KING

During my teenage years, as puberty and peer pressure entered my life, the devotion I had to the Lord faded entirely out of sight. For many years after that, I would serve the world. It was harsh and unforgiving. I made many bad choices and took many wrong turns. Each cost me dearly and wreaked havoc in my life, taking me farther and farther away from the sweet presence of Jesus. Occasionally, I would think of Him and remember those beautiful times I had with Him, but my thoughts would quickly disappear, thinking my life was too far gone to return.

Even so, I still had thoughts of greatness and wondered why I had been born when and where I was. Crying often and dealing with deep-seated feelings of being out of place,

I still did not make a connection to the One who would bring healing.

THE GOD-SHAPED WHOLE YEARNS WITHIN

Having been raised in a solidly upper-middle-class family, one could say I had it all. There was nothing I wanted that daddy would not buy. Through it all, I was empty and devoid of meaning in my life. In my twenties, during the height of the Yuppie Era, I aspired to climb the corporate ladder to obtain wealth and status, hopefully being featured one day on the "Lifestyles of the Rich & Famous." It sounds funny, but many of us longed for that kind of life. It was not until my late twenties that I began to seek meaning. I started thinking about helping people in some way that would make a difference in their lives. I wanted to impact their future and help them become successful. All the materialism of that time could not satisfy the emptiness I felt inside. I wanted change, but I did not know how to get it. I felt trapped in a life I had built for myself that was leading me down a dead-end street. What would I do? How could I get out of this place?

THE KING IS CALLING

The answer I was searching for came from a most unusual place. While attending a corporate seminar on leadership, I noticed a tape all by itself without even a cover. The title was "The Greatest Secret to Success." I had to have it. There must an answer for me here. Surely there would be a key to my future on this tape. I remember hearing so much that day about *dealing with difficult people; success is 99 percent appearance and 1 percent substance, fake it till you make it*. But nothing offered me hope, and all led down the path of deceitful riches.

My mind caught up with my heart that day and made a demand on my future. Literally, my destiny made a demand on my path. As soon as I got into my car, I immediately popped the cassette into the player. As I recall, James Earl Jones narrated. I will never forget the moment when he quoted the Apostle Paul saying, "*For my determined purpose is that I may know Him, that I may become progressively more intimately acquainted with Him perceiving and recognizing His person.*" This statement affected my life so much that I wrote the words down on a piece of paper and taped it to my office computer. It was years before I learned it was a part of Scripture.

James Earl Jones went on to say that the only way anyone could be successful in life was to have a personal relationship with Jesus Christ. God interrupted my life, and from that moment on, I would never be the same.

Those Philippians 3:8-9 passage of Scripture became branded on my heart as I listened daily to the tape. I began to pray those words over my life and asked God to take me into the place He desired me to be, where I could help bring positive change to people's lives.

THE KING TOOK HOLD OF MY HEART

From my heart of compassion and love for all people, God began to open doors and change my career path to bring me into the arena His plan required. Step by step, door by door, I went from a banking administrator to a nonprofit regional director. Then from a crisis pregnancy counselor to an employee of a large church, until I became an itinerant minister, tv/radio host. All the time, I was desiring to do something great for God.

During my tenure on staff at the church, I learned just about every aspect of ministry. My next step took me on a mission trip to Haiti. My first experience in pulpit ministry came while I was there and began to increase as the Lord continued to open more doors. Bible studies and more mission trips, crusades, and prison ministry continued to build my desire to reach a hurting world with the Gospel of Jesus Christ. Once the founder of a nonprofit organization that provides Christ-centered educational programs to women in need. Now I'm an ordained minister who hosts a radio and television program, events, and gatherings leading God's people to a vibrant life in Christ.

THE BEST PART OF LIFE IN THE KING'S COURT

Learning to be a "pray-er" has produced the most incredible wealth and spiritual riches in my life and continues to bring forth growth and intimacy with the Lord. I would rather pray than do most anything. My heart is ever before Him and continually in tune with His prompting.

When I was young in the Lord, I would write out prayer cards and pray specific prayers every day. I remember some of my jewels in prayer began when I learned how to pray the Word of God, take Scripture, and make it personal by inserting my name or another's. As I began to pray this way, I would see an immediate change in situations, which was such a powerful testimony to me as a baby Christian. Answered prayer made me hungry for God's Word and gave me a great desire to declare His Word over myself and others because I had come to know that God watches over His Word to perform it in our life.

Next, I discovered the most beautiful prayer gift that forever changed my life in God—the gift of the Holy Spirit. I love the ministry of the Holy Spirit. Remember Jesus said that He is the Spirit of truth, He will lead and guide us into all truth. We need the ministry of the Holy Spirit to help us in this life. I can testify firsthand of the richness and positive change the Spirit brought into my life when I first received my prayer language. I began to experience the awesome presence of the Lord tangibly. I had more peace and more joy, and I started to see things the way Jesus does. As I prayed in the Spirit, God revealed wisdom I never knew before. I love the Holy Spirit, and because He was such a blessing to me, I wanted more and more of His ministry in my life.

Some of the most powerful times I've had with the Lord as an adult happened when spending time in prayer. There's nothing like His presence; I would not trade anything for it. He is my all and all, nothing else, and no one else will do for me. It's Him and Him alone!

Now I know with such enthusiasm the vital necessity of knowing Christ in my life. Like Paul, it is now my determined purpose that I may know Him, that I may become progressively, more intimately acquainted with Him perceiving and recognizing His person. And more importantly, that I would be known and recognized by all to be His. In Him, I live and move and have my being. Nothing else in this life will make the difference, except Jesus and the work of the Holy Spirit.

I began this journey, searching for the place I had longed for since childhood; the place of greatness, the place of royalty, the place of belonging. I experienced trials and much heartache, but I was determined to live for God, love for Christ, and grow in His ways. He took my hand that day so many years ago and began to lead me on His path, perfecting, molding, and shaping me for His plan.

It has been a journey of much love and joy. I'm thankful for every bend in the road, every rough spot, and every ditch because, in all, He recused me. He brought me back to the place I longed to be, in His arms, cherished and loved, accepted among the beloved. He took my stony heart and gave me a heart of flesh, His *heart* with His love for people. And now this is the place I live from—His heart!

THE ROYAL DAUGHTER IN THE KING'S COURT

After many years, I discovered royalty *is* in my blood. What!?! Yes! I am a daughter of the King, the King of kings. King Jesus is His name. He calls me daughter, a daughter of the King, translated princess. What daughter would have ever thought the desire within her to be a princess was *really* a yearning for God? In this child, it was just that all along. A child of God is the most significant royalty that will ever live on this earth.

The royal daughter, an honorable woman who could care less about the grandeur, pomp, and circumstance that this world has to offer. Now I know what it means to be royalty, and so shall I reign victoriously with my King throughout all eternity in His Court.

Royalty comes out of royal things, and the royal law is to love my God with everything in me and my neighbor as God has loved me. Crusading until the end for others' future, leading them to the Light of Jesus Christ, where they can find acceptance, love, joy, and peace.

TREASURED MOMENTS IN THE KING'S COURT

Today I treasure those moments as a little girl, shut away in my bedroom reading the Bible and meeting with God. That place was the beginning of the end for me. My future was sealed in His hand. I am so grateful for this life He has given me, and I wouldn't trade even one experience, good or bad, because it has all brought me to this place. I am who He says I am, and that is all that matters to me. There is nothing that can compare to the gift He gave in Jesus. He has made me His daughter, a daughter of the King, a princess! I found who I was in the King's court, in the presence of God, and now I reside there with Him.

AN INVITATION TO THE KING'S COURT

I want to invite you to meet my King, Jesus is His name. He will never leave or forsake you and will be the best friend you have ever had. He will do you good all the days of your life. If you don't know my Jesus, pray this prayer with me:

Jesus, I acknowledge that I need help in this life. I'm tired of trying to do everything on my own. I want you to take charge, lead, and guide me in everything I do. I repent of my sins and ask you to come into my heart. Be my Savior and be my Lord. Fill me with your Holy Spirit. I believe you are the Son of God, who died for my sins, and was raised from the dead to live victoriously in heaven with the Father. Help me to live this life for You. Teach me, lead me, guide me, and bring me into the fullness of Your plan for my life. In Jesus' name, I pray. Amen and amen.

JOURNEYING TOGETHER TO THE KING'S COURT

You hold in your hand a book of devotional treasures. I hope they will bless your life as you endeavor to make it your determined purpose to know Him, to become progressively more intimately acquainted with Him perceiving and recognizing His person. Let Him demonstrate His goodness in your life as you learn to trust Him with all your heart. Learn to love Him with all your heart, with all your soul, and with all your strength. If you do this, you will never fail because He will uphold you in everything you do and everything you go through. He is your very best friend, and that's all He ever desired to be!

Now let's turn the page and learn how to live in deep fellowship with our King, from the place of His presence where you will be in constant harmony with Him. Pray and apply what you read, and your life will never be the same again. You, like me, will discover and live from the King's Court.

Chapter One

An Invitation to Greatness

God wants to do something great with your life. He invites you to draw nearer to Him and yield your heart to Him for His purpose. Surrender can sometimes feel scary, but you must allow change to take place in your life to get closer to God. For change to come, you have to let go of what holds you back from Him.

Many years ago, I heard a pastor say, "In the pursuit of one's life purpose, there strategically occurs a *defining moment* in the form of a *refining crisis* setting one free from a *confining limitation*, thus empowering one to step into greatness."

Miriam Webster Dictionary defines "greatness" as a skill marked by *enthusiasm, keenness, eminent, distinguished, or effective.* Someone or something that is superior in character and quality.

To obtain all that God has planned for us, we must endure trials and tests to prepare us for the Master's use. This "refining crisis" or adversity in our lives molds and shapes us into a quality person with a *superior* character.

And here's a simple truth, you have to go *through* something *to* get to something.

We will only accomplish the great things God has designed for us through the adversity we endure in life. Jesus said (John 16:33) that we will have hardship in this world, but He cautioned us, saying be of good cheer for I have overcome the world. Do you know that we can't do more than what Jesus has already done for us?

Paul encouraged us in 2 Corinthians 4:16-17, *"Don't lose heart, even if your outward man is perishing, because the inward man is renewed day by day. For your light and momentary affliction is working for you a far more exceeding and eternal weight of glory."* He further said, don't look at things in the natural and look at the unseen things. In other words, look at your circumstance with spiritual eyes in light of God's promises. The things which you see are temporary and subject to change at any moment. So, don't get caught up in them; look for the fulfillment of God's promises in every situation.

What is that *heavier weight of glory* Paul mentioned? It is a greater awareness of God, a greater dependence upon Him, and a greater level of living in Him. This life is about relationships. It's not a let's make a deal game. I'll do this, so God will do what I want Him to do! He is looking for a friend.

Beloved, we will all be tested as we grow in our friendship with the Lord. No one wants to have adversity, but everyone will. Let's begin to look at our trials differently by changing our perception of adversity to start seeing difficulties as opportunities to grow in God. Hard seasons stretch our faith, causing us to exercise endurance and persevere in the things of God. Times of testing are merely times of preparation. And we all must be prepared for the work of God.

Even Jesus had to prepare for the work God destined Him to perform. In Luke, we see Him baptized in the River Jordan; the Scriptures say that it was at that moment that the Spirit *came upon* Him. Then, when he left the Jordan region, the Scripture says that He *came out filled* with the Spirit. The Scripture explains how the Spirit, Himself, led Jesus into the wilderness where He was tempted and tried by the devil for 40 days, which was Jesus' preparation. After the work was complete, the Scripture says that Jesus *came out in the power* of the Spirit; NOW, wholly prepared for the work ahead.

Jesus had been tried and found to be true by the Father. The word "true" means *steadfast, loyal, honest, just, consistent, narrow, and strict*. These are the same attributes that should be produced in us as we go through trials. Remember, a mark of greatness is to be superior in character and quality. So how do we position ourselves during adversity to produce these characteristics?

When all hell breaks loose against us, we stand and declare God's goodness and faithfulness. No matter what, we will speak life and blessing. Declare who God is and what He will do in the situation. By doing this, we will withstand the enemy. We will overcome. We will see the victory we are promised.

Our posture in crisis is face-up, eyes closed, and hands lifted! Lift your eyes to the hills from where your help comes. Your help comes in the name of the Lord. Stay focused on Him who is the Author and Finisher of our faith. He will bring to completion the work He has begun. Remember, all things are working together for our good, so lift those holy hands and worship the Lord.

Another vital key in adversity, stay quiet! A hard lesson to learn, but I promise you God is better able to take care of your situation than you are. So many times, we want to defend ourselves or to tell everyone what happened. The moment we open our mouths and start speaking about the situation, we bind the hand of God. If we were quiet, God would take up our cause and defend us.

I remember a couple of my circumstances that happened many years ago. The first was a simple thing. We needed to landscape our yard. I'd been asking my husband to do it for a long time. I was so aggravated about it that I began to speak sarcastically to him. I remember telling God about it in prayer one day. The Holy Spirit spoke immediately back to me, saying, "Why don't you ask Me to tell him, instead of you hounding him about it?" Wow, what an epiphany! I asked the Holy Spirit to tell my husband about it right then. Do you know, within a couple of days, my husband said he had contacted a landscaper! And within a few weeks, it was done. I'd droned on and on about it for so long, stressing and pressuring him instead of asking God. Watch what you say in every situation and who you ask to get involved. The best solution is to ask God. He will work it out so much quicker and easier than you ever can.

The second circumstance was much more severe. In this one, I had several brothers and sisters in the Lord attack my character because God revealed an issue regarding a detrimental matter they were involved in that involved the church. After much prayer, I did exactly what

God asked me to do in the situation. Because the attack came through the actions of fellow believers, it was devastating. I remember weeping and crying out to God, saying, "I did what you told me to do! See what has happened!!!" I asked God to trouble the heart of the king (my pastor) regarding the issue, just like He did in Esther's day regarding the deeds of Mordecai, which ultimately saved the king's life. I asked Him not to allow the people to sleep who had falsely accused me. And, I diligently prayed that truth would prevail. What I did not do was tell everyone who would listen about what had happened. I stayed quiet!

Don't you know that God did trouble the heart of the king, and within a couple of days, one of the individuals who falsely accused me came back to me and said, "I could not sleep all night!"

I was amazed! God had proven Himself just and true in my case. He will uphold *you* in times of trouble too. And if you let Him do the speaking, He will defend and deliver you in a more fantastic way than anything or anyone else could.

Let's face it, though, sometimes we think the enemy is attacking us, but what we thought was adversity was the mercy and grace of God trying to perfect our character. We can't change anything in our life. We can exert our will, but real, lasting change without ever having to deal with wrestling our will only come through a supernatural change brought through the power of the Holy Spirit. We often don't know we need to change until our issues are brought to the surface. Mercy brings the truth to the forefront of our minds. Once we acknowledge the problem and repent, God's grace is made available to overcome. Always be willing to examine your own heart in everything that happens. Don't assume it's someone else or the devil; sometimes, you need to surrender.

A powerful position to take in adversity is to remain joyful. Why did James say to count it all joy when you fall into various trials? As did all of the other disciples, he knew firsthand that the testing of your faith produces patience.

And, when patience is realized, you will be complete, lacking nothing. Nehemiah 8:10 tells us that joy is your strength. Joy is just what you need to carry you through. So, I say to you; it's time to rejoice. It's time to rejoice!

Joy is the indicator of your strength. Proverbs 24:10 says, *"If you faint in the day of adversity, your strength is small."* In other words, if you faint in adversity, you have lost your joy and your faith!

In Corinthians, Paul said, "I am exceedingly joyful in tribulation." Joy is a stronghold, a fortified place against the enemy. Maintaining your joy will cause you to withstand the enemy and carry you over to victory. Fight to keep your joy because it's the first thing the enemy wants to steal. It's like a wall of defense, and every time you lose joy, the wall comes down, making you vulnerable.

So remember, during a defining moment when adversity comes, God is moving in the midst of it. He's perfecting, molding, and shaping you into the person He's called you to be. He wants you to become superior in character and quality. He wants you to be marked by the greatness that brings many to the knowledge of Christ.

Pray this: Father, I recognize that the purpose of my tests and trials are to mold and shape me into the person You have created me to be in this life. I will remain faithful and true to You allowing You to work on my behalf. Fill me with joy and assurance that You are bringing to pass the things You have designed for me. I take my hands off of every person and situation, relinquishing each to Your mighty hand. In Jesus' name I pray. Amen!

Chapter Two

Destiny Makes Demand

There comes the point in everyone's life where we realize we are stagnant, unfulfilled, or empty. We wake up one morning and look around, realizing there is more to life.

I know, it happened to me in 1990, following many years of working in the financial sector. Frustration was building; uneasiness flourished in my soul, then came a series of resounding questions from my heart;

- Am I helping anyone?
- Am I making a difference in the world?
- In my community?
- In people's lives?
- In my own life and family?

As I thoughtfully answered each of these questions, I had to admit I was not making much impact anywhere. Wow, what a revelation! A definite defining moment!

Immediately I began to desire something different. I started looking around me and considering my options. What could I do? Where could I go? How could I help others?

These moments often happen in the lives of God's people. Psalm 139 reveals to us that God numbered our days before we were in our mother's womb. He already knew everything about you and prepared a life of blessing for you. He has a destiny in store for all who will surrender themselves to Him for His purpose.

As I meditated on this revelation, the awesomeness of our Father's love flooded my soul. His footsteps have prepared our way, so we need to follow Him.

Before we come to the knowledge of plan and purpose, we meander through life, going in all directions, stopping, stumbling, falling, totally oblivious to what God is doing. But think for a moment; if God numbered your days, then

He prepared your path, and the Holy Spirit is walking with you continually trying to get you to turn and follow God on His prepared pathway.

It was the Holy Spirit's prompting that day when I woke up and asked the question: Am I really making a difference?

Not long after that pivotal moment, my employer sent me to one of those professional seminars. You might have been to one before. They are like a rally of speakers telling you how to be successful in business!

Even though my heart was already changing and I stood at the big decisions threshold, I agreed to attend this seminar. It was a typical seminar on business success; "fake it till you make it!" and "success is 99% appearance." Empty, dead, devoid of authenticity and truth! I left more determined than ever to transition away from this shallow life of appearances.

On my way out, I walked by the tape table and noticed a single tape sitting on the edge of the table. Do you know how uncommon this is for these types of seminars? I mean really, one of the primary purposes of these seminars is to sell volumes of material. It was so unusual for a single cassette tape to be available. I remember thinking how odd it was that this one tape was sitting there by itself. I picked it up, looked at it. I thought how interesting it was. The message on the cassette tape was entitled, "The Greatest Secret to Success." Well, I thought, I have two hours to drive home. I might as well listen to it.

After purchasing the tape, I left, got to my car, jumped in, and pushed the tape into the player to listen. To my surprise, the message about the SECRET to success was a personal relationship with Jesus Christ! Wow!

I remember one phrase hitting my heart, an expression that would profoundly change my path and my life forever. "For my determined purpose is that I may know Him, become progressively more intimately acquainted with Him perceiving and recognizing His person."

When I heard that "phrase," I had no idea it was Philippians 3:8 & 9. This Scripture became the banner of my life. It is who I am today and my greatest desire.

Imagine my amazement years later when I realized the very "phrase" that changed my life years earlier was actually Paul exhorting Christians to a deeper awareness of Christ.

I didn't know then, but this taped message was peppered with Scripture from the Bible. I listened to the message over and over again. It pierced my heart so deeply that I wrote it down on Sticky Notes and posted it on my office computer.

I also responded to the message as I sought a deeper relationship with the Lord. And, I began looking for another job, one that would catapult me into a life given to helping others. Every day I trusted God to take me down the pathway of His will.

When I think back on that time in my life, I am totally amazed at the awesomeness of God. He stopped me dead in my tracks that day and completely changed my direction. An incredible journey began by following God step by step and allowing Him to teach, train, and prepare me for every new adventure in His plan.

Destiny made a demand on my path, and I was never the same afterward. God interrupted me and turned me around. I opened the door to Him by acknowledging that I wanted to do something to help people. A very simple request, but when I made it, He came in and took over.

There is more that God wants to do in your life too. There is a destiny that God planned for you before the foundation of the earth; before you were formed in your mother's womb. And, rest assured, if you are in the wrong place today, your destiny will make a demand on your path to bring you into the fullness of God's plan for you!

Open the door to Him with a simple prayer.

Pray this: Lord, lead me to the path You have prepared for my life! Now trust Him, obey Him, and follow. Miracles await you.

Chapter Three

Times of Preparation

It is said that Jesus went from place of prayer to place of prayer with miracles in between. Prayer is what prepared Jesus to walk in the power of the Spirit, and it is what will prepare us to walk in the power of the Spirit where we will see miracles.

For example, when John the Baptist baptized Jesus in the River Jordan, Luke 3:22 says, *"the Holy Spirit descended upon Jesus..."* And, when Jesus returned from the Jordan, Luke 4:1 says, *"Jesus was filled with the Spirit."*

Then the SPIRIT led Jesus into the wilderness where the devil tempted him for forty days (verse 2.) Notice it was the Spirit of God that led Jesus into the wilderness, where He ate no food. He fasted and prayed for 40 days.

These moments were necessary for Jesus' time of preparation. He could not forsake it; it was required of Him to prepare Him for what was to come.

This same preparation is also required of believers. It is not to be feared or forsaken.

Preparation is simply a time taken to make someone ready for use. Part of the word preparation is "pare," which means;

- to take out what is not necessary
- to trim off the outside, excess or irregular parts
- to diminish

The meaning brings to mind what John the Baptist said to his followers regarding Jesus, "*He must increase, but I must decrease*" (John 3:30). Don't you know Jesus was saying the same thing to the Father while He was in the wilderness? I must decrease so that You, Father, can increase in Me.

The word "prepared" means to;

- put in a proper state of mind
- work out the details

- plan in advance

The word "compound" is a synonym of the word "prepared," which means; *to combine several parts to make a whole.* Your seasons of preparation are times when you are made one with the Spirit of God.

We don't know everything that happened to Jesus in the wilderness, but we know the devil followed Him there and tempted Him. These events tried Him and made Him ready for the Master's use.

The word "tried" means: *to be found good, faithful, and trustworthy through experience and testing.*

While you keep all these facts in your mind, let's look at the result of Jesus' time of preparation in the wilderness.

Luke 4:14 says, "When Jesus returned from the wilderness, He returned in the Power of the Spirit." He was now ready to do what prayer had prepared Him to do; miracles, signs, and wonders.

Look at the progression of the Spirit developing Jesus' life. First, the Spirit was upon Him, then the Spirit-filled

Him, and after a set apart time of preparation, He came out in the Power of the Spirit.

I always hear people say, "I want to see the hand of God move." I have an answer for them: If you want to see the hand of God move, pray. And if you want to move the hand of God through prayer, prepare yourself and enter in so that you can be prepared when you come out to see and participate with the power of God.

Part of preparation requires prayer. Praying in the Spirit strengthens you. Prayer prepares you to walk in POWER of the Spirit.

Do not forsake these times of preparation, whether it's forty days or four, forty hours or four, forty minutes or four. Prepare yourself by setting your heart on things above, and empty yourself of you, so that God can fill you with Him.

It's time for you to walk in the Power of the Spirit, from place of prayer to place of prayer, experiencing miracles in between.

Afterall, miracles are answered prayer!

Pray this: Father, prepare me to walk in the power of the Spirit. I surrender my heart and mind now to You. Completely inhabit my life and thoughts. Have Your way in me in Jesus' name, amen.

Chapter Four

Walk in the Spirit

Paul boldly exhorts us in Galatians 5 verses 16 through 25 to walk in the Spirit. He reveals to us that when we do, we will not fulfill the lust of the flesh. He goes on to say, "*For the flesh lusts against the Spirit, and the Spirit against the flesh; and these are contrary to one another, so that you do not do the things that you wish. But if you are led by the Spirit, you are not under the law.*"

While he describes the lust of the flesh in detail, we believers are to take heed to our lives, repenting and removing any lust described in Scripture. As we let go of the old lustful nature, we will walk in the Spirit, becoming more Christ-like toward everyone around us.

The attributes produced as evidence that we are walking in the Spirit are the fruit of the Spirit:

- love
- joy
- peace
- longsuffering
- kindness
- goodness
- faithfulness
- gentleness
- self-control.

The fruit of the Spirit is also a picture of the nature of God. Everything contained therein is also a fruit or character attribute of the God we serve, and as we are transformed into His image, that same nature is being birthed in us as we become more like Jesus.

When you are first born again, love is the biggest thing. It's the whole reason you found salvation. *Love* opened the doorway of eternity to you, and the outworking of love in your life will open the doorway to greater levels of walking in the Spirit.

Once love was accepted, joy filled our soul because of the grace we received. Oh, how joyful we are when we know that grace covers our sin. Then peace is produced out of a quiet assurance that your future is secure.

So, you can see how one fruit builds upon another as we progress in our relationship with our heavenly Father. Love is what everything else is built upon, and without it, we are a clanging cymbal to the Lord.

No wonder "self-control" is the last fruit listed because it is the believer's lifelong pursuit to have more self-control. The more we grow in this fruit, the more we become like our elder brother Jesus.

As we consider the fruit of the flesh and the fruit of the Spirit, it becomes easy to determine where we are in our walk! All we have to do is gauge our hearts. Ask a few questions. Am I jealous, contentious, angry, etc.? If so, you need to turn back to Jesus and walk in the Spirit.

Paul perfectly explained how we should respond when we realize we are walking in the flesh in his letter to the

Colossians, verses 3:10-17 describes how to put on the new man.

PUT ON THE NEW MAN who is renewed in knowledge according to the image of Him who created him.

"Therefore, as the elect of God, holy and beloved, put on tender mercies, kindness, humility, meekness, longsuffering; bearing with one another, and forgiving one another, if anyone has a complaint against another; even as Christ forgave you, so you also must do. But above all these things put on love, which is the bond of perfection. And let the peace of God rule in your hearts, to which also you were called in one body; and be thankful. Let the word of Christ dwell in you richly in all wisdom, teaching and admonishing one another in psalms and hymns and spiritual songs, singing with grace in your hearts to the Lord. And whatever you do in word or deed, do all in the name of the Lord Jesus, giving thanks to God the Father through Him."

Our walk is progressive. Step by step, growth takes place. We can see how God produces that growth in our life by the pruning of the vine. Whatever vine is producing good fruit will be pruned slightly to encourage more growth.

In the process of learning to walk in the Spirit, we are growing in the fruit of the Spirit. When tests come, the pruning begins as we learn to respond rightly in trials. Pruning equals humility. The further we humble ourselves, the more fruit is produced. God has appointed us, or chosen us, to bear fruit, the kind of fruit that remains forever in our life (John 15:16).

Trees yield fruit in season. Let's look figuratively at our lives. When a season of victory comes, it produces joy. When a season of testing comes, it produces patience, longsuffering, and self-control. Whatever season you are in, you should be bearing fruit. The fruit that remains and increases prepares you for the next season of your life. Don't fight your circumstances; learn to live in them and be content no matter what.

The life of Mary is an excellent example of fruit being produced.

"And she (Mary) offered no resistance. She could have. 'Who am I to have God in my womb? I'm not good enough,' she could have said. Or, 'I've got other plans. I don't have time for God in my life.' But Mary didn't say such words. Instead, she said, 'Behold, the bond-slave of the Lord; may it be done to me according to your word" (Luke 1:38).

Max Lucado once wrote, "If Mary is our measure, God seems less interested in talent and more interested in trust. Unlike her, we tend to assist God, assuming our part is as important as His. Or we resist, thinking we are too bad or too busy. Yet when we assist or resist, we miss God's great grace. We miss out on the reason we were placed on earth—to be so pregnant with heaven's child that He lives through us. To be so full of Him that we could say with Paul, "It is no longer I who live, but Christ lives in me" (Galatians 2:20).

Becoming more Christ-like is the ultimate purpose of walking in the Spirit. The fullness of Him and God's nature produced by a life yielded to the master for the expressed purpose of being prepared for His use.

Fruit is the blessing and nourishment of what a tree produces. Isaiah called believers "trees of righteousness" for a reason. This reference is a perfect metaphor because we produce spiritual fruit in our life as we walk in the Spirit with the Lord. The fruit of the Spirit that blesses and nourishes everyone around us.

Chapter Five

Be Led by the Spirit

Psalm 37:23 tells us that the Lord orders the steps of a good man. God established and ordered our steps before the foundation of the earth (Psalm 139). The only challenge believers have is uncovering the steps as they endeavor to walk with God.

The word "ordered" in Psalm 37:23 means *to reveal*. God reveals each step, one at a time. How does He do this? Everything that we need from God comes out of the Spirit. Zechariah 4:6 boldly declares, *"not by might, nor by power, but by My Spirit says the Lord of Hosts."* And Romans 8 tells us that the children of God are lead by the Spirit of God.

God leads us by His Spirit.

God is a communicating Father. He wants to talk with His children, and His preferred method of communication is direct to the one who needs the information. Interestingly, the word commune is found in communication.

We must commune or spend time in the presence of the one with whom we are communicating. If we need information from God as to our position or next step, we will have to spend time with Him to communicate it to us.

All of God's plans and purposes are revealed by Holy Spirit. Praying in the Spirit will allow the supernatural processes of God to reveal to us His plans and purposes for our life; walking in the Spirit, living in the Spirit, being led by the Spirit.

You are your best resource with God and the Holy Spirit! God has already given you all things that pertain to life and godliness (2 Peter 1:3). Now you have to learn how to dig it up, uncover the steps, and bring the details to the surface so that the information will be of benefit in your life.

Proverbs 20:5 gives us a clue about how this works for God's children. "Counsel in the heart of man is like deep water, but a man of understanding will draw it out." God's fingerprint is upon your heart, and the blueprint of His plan is within you. How does this man or woman draw out the counsel of the Lord from the heart?

We tap into our heart by praying in the Spirit. Jude 20 declares, "But you, beloved, building yourselves up on your most holy faith, praying in the Holy Spirit..."

Jude is saying here that when we pray in the Spirit, we are building up our faith. We are strengthening ourselves and positioning ourselves to receive instruction from God, as well as digging up and uncovering the information we need for every situation.

We should carefully build ourselves up. We should take care to do this. It's a vital part of a believer's life, and we should take time to pray in the Spirit daily.

The New Living Translation defines this as "... *continue to build your lives on the foundation of your holy faith. And continue to pray as the Holy Spirit directs you.*"

The Holy Spirit directs us in our prayer. He will lead and guide our prayer to ensure that the perfect will of the Father is brought forth and realized in your life.

The phrase "building up" literally means:

- house-builder
- construct
- confirm
- edify
- embolden
- to build upon.

Praying in the Spirit builds or strengthens our "spirit house," construct, confirm God's plan for us, edify us, and cause us to be bold in the Lord.

The Holy Spirit is the agent of action of the God Head. He does the will of the Father, and He brings to pass the plans of God. He leads and guides us. The Holy Spirit is the muscle and the breath of God. We give breath to His words as we pray in the Spirit, and the perfect will of God is brought to pass.

Pray in the Spirit, be led by the Spirit. Yield yourself to His prompting, and He will lead and guide you into the center of God's will; edifying you, building you up, and confirming it all to you as you endeavor to walk the path God has prepared for your life.

Chapter Six

Expressions of God

Our life is an expression. No matter how good or how bad our life may be, it expresses something to everyone around us. Our lives should be an expression of God's divine nature. 2 Corinthians 2, verses 14 and 15 reveal the fragrance of the knowledge of God diffuses itself through us to those who are being saved and to those who are perishing. The word diffuse in Greek means *to appear*. It also means *to manifest, to show, and to declare.*

Our ultimate destiny in Christ is to be transformed into His image. As we go through this transformation, our life is expressing more and more the knowledge of God. As we grow in Him, our life is diffusing the fragrance of His knowledge more and more to everyone around us. Another meaning of diffuse is to spread out wide. In other words, our life will become known to many. Or, you could say, Christ will become known to many through our way of living. Have you ever been around someone who just seemed to invoke in you a certain feeling or emotion for the Lord? If so, it happened because of the fragrance of the knowledge of God that diffused from them. This will also come to pass in your life as you grow in God more and more.

Paul made a remarkable statement in Ephesians 5. He said in verse 2, *"Live a life filled with love for others, following the example of Christ, who loved you and gave Himself as a sacrifice to take away your sins. And God was pleased, because that sacrifice was like sweet perfume to Him"* (NLT). Paul tells us exactly how to develop your life into a full expression of God. Live a life filled with love for others. Be an example of Christ. As you do this, your life will be a "sweet perfume" or fragrance to Him. And it's implied that you would be that same fragrance to everyone around you, diffusing the fragrance of the knowledge of God, which happens when we know Him. Knowledge is to know; therefore, as we come into closer fellowship with our Father, the fragrance, or sweet-smelling aroma, will increase in us as we increase in our knowledge of Him.

I love to be around people who have personal knowledge of the goodness of God. Those who seem to walk close to Him. When they speak, it feels as though God Himself stepped into the room. When they come close, you feel as though the Lord came with them. God desires this life for each of us, that we would know Him and grow in our knowledge of Him day by day, moment by moment. How do we come to know someone? We spend time with them. So, to grow in this knowledge of God and grow in the diffusion of His fragrance, we must spend time with Him.

Read His Word, pray always, and sit in His presence. Be still and know our God. As we do these things, our lives will become a true expression of Him, and everyone around us will sense and know that He is with us.

Chapter Seven

The Benefits of Surrender

God created you for fellowship, first with Him.

We will never be completely satisfied until we give our all to Him. If we were to yield to Him fully provide our every thought and action to His service the way He chooses, there would-be never-ending joy. A life full of Him is a life fully yielded and seeking after His plan and purpose.

He chose you. You did not choose Him. When you yielded to His prompting, He set a seal upon you - the Holy Spirit. As 2 Corinthians 1:20-22 declares, *"It is God who makes both us and you stand firm in Christ. He anointed us, set his seal of ownership on us, and put his Spirit in our hearts as a deposit, guaranteeing what is to come."* (NIV)

Ephesians 1:13-14 further reveals, *"And you also were included in Christ when you heard the word of truth, the gospel of your salvation. Having believed, you were marked in him with a seal, the promised Holy Spirit."* (NIV)

Isn't it "wonder-full" to know that we are sealed and guaranteed by our Creator?

Because He has given so much to us in Christ, it is a little thing to expect us to give ourselves back to Him - not withholding any part of us, but with reckless abandon throwing ourselves headlong into Him.

Paul called this our "reasonable service." The picture he painted of this act is that we present our bodies as a living sacrifice holy and pleasing to God (Romans 12:1).

Because of this, we should live and walk holy and humbly before our God. He directed us in Leviticus 11:44 to, *"...consecrate yourselves and be holy, because I am holy."* And the Apostle Peter said our life should be shaped by Jesus' life, which will only come to pass as we live with a deep awareness of Him.

God is waiting for us to cast off the world with reckless abandon and determined ourselves to walk into His wonderful plan. He has designed so many amazing things for each of us. He wants us to be like little children on Christmas morning, living every moment with that same great anticipation and excitement.

So eager we couldn't sleep all night, because we can't wait to get out of bed to see what new and marvelous thing, He has prepared for us this day. Then live each day as though it would be our last, paying attention to every detail of love, every moment of thanks, and filling our hearts with joy, knowing that we will see Him soon.

God desires our lives to be given for His service, that He may live through us to demonstrate His goodness to a desperate world full of such darkness. More simply put, He needs our life to live through so that His nature will be seen.

I am confident that if we were to perceive the great things He wants to do entirely, we would immediately throw down our schedules and abandon everything to be a small part of His plan. It is marvelous and full of wonder! You don't want to miss a moment of it.

Don't miss one more day!

Tell God you want to give your all to Him for His plan, then lay down your life and start acting like Him so that the world will see Him through you.

Chapter Eight

Full Surrender!

"The eyes of the LORD search the whole earth in order to strengthen those whose hearts are fully committed to him." (2 Chronicles 16:9)

God is looking for willing and loyal believers. Why? He wants to strengthen them! He wants to show Himself mighty on their behalf!

The original English version (The Geneva Bible 1499) reads, *"them that are of perfect heart toward him…"* This "perfect heart" according to the Hebrew word "shalem" is *completely devoted to God.* Not "perfect" in actions, fully surrendered to the Lord for His hand of perfection to work in the heart to bring the believer to full stature in Christ.

God is always at work by the influence of Holy Spirit to bring you to this completion so that you will be strong! He continues this work every single day, no matter what you are doing.

His work transforms you into a full expression of the Divine nature of Christ. In this expression, you choose to respond in every situation and circumstance the same way Jesus did, fulfilling His words in John 15:19. "I only do what I see My Father do."

As you begin the process, you may not respond correctly. It takes time in this transformation. The mark of growth is recovery time. What used to take years will begin to take months, weeks, or days. As we come to full stature, it takes moments for us to adjust ourselves to Christlikeness. Next, we automatically surrender to His way, responding immediately the way Jesus would in any given situation. Praise God for His work in our hearts.

I love what God said to Solomon in 1 Chronicles 28:9 and 10, *"And you, Solomon my son, know the God of your father [have personal knowledge of Him, be acquainted with, and understand Him; appreciate, heed, and cherish Him] and serve him with a blameless heart and a willing mind. For the Lord searches all hearts and minds and understands all the wanderings of the thoughts. If you seek Him [inquiring for and of Him and requiring Him as your first and vital necessity] you will find Him...take heed now, for the Lord has chosen you to build a house for the sanctuary. Be strong and do it."*

This verse reveals that God understands your thoughts and concerns, but it also declares the call. You are called to build the Kingdom of God on earth. When God says, "Be strong and do it," I receive this as God simply saying, get out of yourself, get into the Spirit, and allow My strength to finish the work. And, realize this, it's not just about what you are doing individually. It's also about what you are doing as one body for the Kingdom.

Solomon speaks back to God, declaring his heart, "*O LORD our God, all this abundance that we have prepared to build You a house for Your holy name is from Your hand, and is all Your own. I know also, my God, that You test the heart and have pleasure in uprightness. As for me, in the uprightness of my heart I have willingly offered all these things."* (1 Chronicles 29:16,17a)

God is watching out for those who are willing, those whose hearts are fully devoted and surrendered to Him. He is searching for these to strengthen them and do wonderful things on their behalf.

Make the decision today to be loyal to Him. Be quick to respond according to His Word and ways. Look for opportunities to demonstrate these qualities of character to Him, then you will reap the benefits of full surrender, and you will have the strength of the Lord for everything that comes your way in life!

Chapter Nine

The Blessing of Doing

I often remind people that knowledge is gained from education, understanding is garnered through applied knowledge, and wisdom is the result. In the kingdom of God, this is applied as we do what we learn from the Scriptures.

James 1:25 boldly declares that those who do not forget what they have learned but become doers of it, they will be blessed in what they do. Paul further encourages us in Philippians 4:9, saying, *"The things which you learned and received and heard and saw in me, these do, and the God of peace will be with you."* I love this Scripture because it comes with a promise. When you do these things, not only will God be with you, but you will have peace!

It's up to us to put into practice the things that Jesus, His apostles, and followers taught us. Paul declared boldly in 1 Corinthians 1:2 that all the promises of God in Him are "yes" and "amen," which means each one is given to us in full.

We can walk in them and experience all the goodness and abundance God provided. There is one caveat, we must become doers of the Word. God didn't just promise us a good life. He instructed us on how to live it.

Many times, we refuse to walk in God's ways and then blame Him when things don't go well. It is now time for each of us to examine our own lives, to see if we are true followers, truly imitators, true believers of the highest God.

The Word of God has an answer for every situation that could come up in this life. If you don't know what God has to say about something, then become a student of the Word. Ask the Holy Spirit, who is the teacher, to lead and guide you into all truth.

Jesus said in Luke 6:40 that everyone who is fully trained would be like his teacher, which is what we should all aspire to be, just like our teacher. The Word reveals in Romans 8:29 that God predestined us to be conformed into the image of His Son. It happens as we learn more and more about who He is and what He has done, then we put into practice the same things that He did, becoming faithful followers.

Our part in this is to hear the Word and do it. When we become doers of the Word, we will be blessed, and God will demonstrate His goodness through us as a beautiful sign to the world. But remember, God is not looking for a robot. He is looking for a relationship, one between the Father and His children. That's why Paul encouraged us in Ephesians 5:1 to be imitators of God as dear children. God created us for fellowship, and by spending time with Him, through His Word and prayer, we will become more and more like Him.

Peter summed all this up so perfectly in 2 Peter 1:2—11. These verses are excellent because they give specific instructions about how we participate in God's blessed plans and escape the corruption of evil in the world. Here's a summarized list:

- Be full of faith and God's goodness
- Receive the knowledge of God, exercise self-control

- Be longsuffering, godly, kind, and full of unconditional love
- Possess these qualities in increasing measure

We do this by practice, repeatedly; as we give ourselves to this, we are learning, living, and walking in God's way.

Take on the role of student/child and sit at the feet of Jesus as you read His Word. Then do whatever the Word shows you to do! Put into practice what you learn, and experience the blessings and goodness God has planned for your life!

If you do these things, you will NEVER fail, you will be blessed, and you will be full of the peace of God!

Chapter Ten

Guarding Your Gates

Proverbs 4:23-26 says, *"Keep [and guard] your heart with all diligence [and above all that you guard], for out of it spring [flow] the issues of life. Put away from you [false and dishonest speech and willful and contrary talk] a deceitful mouth, and put perverse lips far from you. Let your eyes look straight ahead [with fixed purpose], and your eyelids look right before you. Ponder the path of your feet, and let all your ways be established [and ordered aright]."* (AMP)

It is no wonder that on the heels of telling us to guard our hearts, the Scripture then mentions the mouth and eyes. These are the heart's avenues, the ways by which corrupt information gets in and comes out. And, in addition to the eyes and mouth, ears are another avenue to the heart that must be secured.

We should maintain with watchful purpose a strict hand on the things we open our spirit up to through conversation, television, reading, etc. In doing so, we will keep our souls from corruption and remain pure and infallible in our dealings with ourselves and others.

The life of God resides on the inside of us. So take heed to your spirit, and maintain holy jealousy for yourself by setting a strict guard on all the soul's avenues - the eyes, ears, and mouth.

Keep your heart from hurting others and getting hurt, from being defiled by sin and disturbed by trouble. Keep your heart as your jewel, as your vineyard, steering clear of offense, staving off wrong thoughts; making sure you are consumed with good thoughts. Keep your affections set on the right things and in due bounds.

Look straight ahead, keeping your eyes set only on the Lord, putting your hand to the plow and not looking either to the right or left. Then let everything you see, hear, or say be metered or weighed by the Word of God. Put every situation on the scale of God's Word and see if it agrees or is balanced by what you are seeing, hearing, or want to say. If it doesn't balance, then don't allow it into your heart or out of your mouth. We should never be hasty in our actions, but steady, consistent, and cautious, walking circumspectly before our God.

Proverbs 19:2 teaches us that we sin when we allow our feet to be hastened away. In other words, we don't take the time to think about what we are doing but rather jump headlong into it. We miss the mark many times and cause false steps to be taken in haste. When we consider our actions and weigh them with the Word of God, then we will walk circumspectly, meaning to guard, take heed and watch with diligence staying close to God on the path He established.

When we don't guard our hearts, we open ourselves up to all kinds of inappropriate things that will ultimately cost us dearly by keeping us from the full blessing of God.

It reminds me of a revelation the Holy Spirit once gave to me. Over the years, I have served the church as a leader in prayer ministry. I remember hearing people talk about going to R-rated movies. These were believers - friends of mine who I love. I remember there was a pressure to yield to their way.

One day, I considered watching a movie that was not appropriate, and the Holy Spirit checked me, "Do not think that you will watch such things and enter into the holy presence of God in prayer." My consideration was halted immediately; nothing was worth the tremendous price of losing intimacy with God.

Another situation also comes to mind. My husband and I once attended a party at a church friend's house. During the party, there was a lot of conversation about intimate issues between couples. I was taken back and told my husband that I would not enter into such discussions because I felt they were inappropriate.

My words got back to one of the individuals who then called me a prude. At first, I was hurt, but then the Holy

Spirit revealed that a prude is prudent. Proverbs 8:12 tells us that wisdom dwells with prudence. People can call me what they want, but I will not subject my spirit to things that will open the door to sin and destruction.

If we stay hooked up with the Holy Spirit and walk in the light according to God's way, we will gain access to places few have ever walked. We will become consumed with the plans and purposes of the Lord and be like arrows in the hand of God to be shot forth throughout the earth. The life of God will flow out of our hearts and affect everything and everyone around us.

Keep your heart with all diligence; keep it for God alone. Keep it hidden from the world, and do not allow defilement to enter, in any form. When you do this, God will see that He can trust you with great things.

Chapter Eleven

Eyes Up!

So many times, in the lives of believers, we get bogged down with circumstances. We carry burdens and weights for things God never asked us to bear. He instructed us to cast our care upon Him so that He could care for us.

When we are heavily laden with the cares of this life, we should lift our eyes toward heaven and ask God to take care of our every need. Colossians 3 instructs us well;

"Seek those things which are above, where Christ is, sitting at the right hand of God. Set your mind on things above, not on things on the earth. For you died, and your life is hidden with Christ in God."

Think of Paul's statement above and receive the reality, when we focus on things above, we are hidden with Christ. Powerful revelation! Then Psalm 31:19b and 20 shows us something equally impressive;

"...which You have prepared for those who trust in You in the presence of the sons of men. You shall hide them in the secret place of Your presence, from the plots of man. You shall keep them secretly in a pavilion from the strife of tongues."

When we place our trust in God, He will hide us in HIS secret place! Now I don't know about you, but that makes my heart LEAP! HIS secret place, a pavilion, meaning in Greek, *"encased."* He safely protects us from the plots of man and the strife of tongues.

As we keep our eyes fixed securely on Him, we prove we trust Him alone with everything in our life.

Here's another thought. Our life unfolds in the direction of our focus. If your focus is on your circumstance, you will go the way of the flesh and overcome the situation. If you are focused on the Lord, you will go in the direction of God and walk in the Spirit to victory over your circumstance.

And, even though we might be a blessed and prosperous people, we should not place our focus on our riches either (Psalm 62:10), but on Jesus, who is the author and finisher of our faith. Christ Who opened and provided a door to us, and by Him alone, all things exist.

Never put your trust in riches, in your flesh, or the strength of men. All will surely pass away; each is fading and false. Put your trust in Him who can do above and beyond anything you could ever ask, desire, imagine or dream (Ephesians 3:20).

Are you hidden today? If you keep your mind on the things above, you will be hidden with Christ. You will be tucked safely away in the secret place of His presence, literally hidden from the enemy.

It's so simple keep your mind set on Him!

Chapter Twelve

Anxiety be Gone!

Our intimacy with God determines our level of anxiety. In other words, when your life in God is more focused on circumstance than His promises or provision, then you will be anxious about everything. But when you cultivate your life in God to the point that NOTHING will cause you to get your eyes off Jesus, then and only then will you walk above your circumstance and realize the full provision and promises of God that bring peace and blessing in every area of your life.

Philippians 4:4-9 says, *"Rejoice in the Lord always. Again, I will say, rejoice! Let your gentleness be known to all men. The Lord is at hand. Be anxious for nothing, but in everything by prayer and supplication, with thanksgiving, let your requests be made known to God;*

and the peace of God, which surpasses all understanding, will guard your hearts and minds through Christ Jesus."

I find it interesting that Paul would tell us to rejoice right before telling us to be anxious for nothing. Joy is so powerful and the word "rejoice" literally means to *re-joy*. Make sure that your joy is full by continually filling yourself up with joy. How is it that we lose our joy? And when we lose it, how do we get it back? Let's look at a few key questions.

First, what are you thinking about at that moment? Whatever you set your mind on will determine your anxiety level. If you place your mind on the circumstance and meditate on the problem, you will be anxious. However, suppose you set your mind on the ability of God and what God has said. In that case, you will lose your anxiety and become joyful at the expectation of God doing something extraordinary concerning your situation. Here's an example. If I receive a bad report regarding my health and begin to focus on it, I would be afraid of the possible outcome.

On the other hand, if I receive a bad report and I remind myself of God's promise concerning sickness, disease, and infirmity, I will declare my healing and be happy about God's promise for the outcome. Notice I mentioned that I have to remind myself. We should keep God's promises close because we never know when we will need to remind ourselves about them. Once we remind ourselves of His promise, we will also have to meditate on that promise to keep it in our hearts. We do this to replace the thoughts of fear and apprehension with thoughts of God's promise of victory.

Another key question is, what are you talking about at that moment? Are you talking about the current situation, or are you calling those things that are not as though they were? 2 Corinthians 5:7 declares That we walk by faith and not by sight! Faith calls those things that are not as though they are. And further, 2 Corinthians 4:16—18 instructs us, *"...do not lose heart. Even though our outward man is perishing, yet the inward man is being renewed day by day. For our light affliction, which is but for a moment, is working for us a far more exceeding and eternal weight of glory, while we do not look at the things which are seen, but at the things which are not seen. For the things which are seen are temporary, but the things which are not seen are eternal."*

What does this Scripture reveal? Our situation is temporary and subject to change at any moment. If you are talking about the problem's weight and not realizing it will change eventually, you will become weighed down. If you don't believe the situation will change, then ultimately, you will lose hope. But if you remind yourself that God is working all things together for good and begin talking about what He is doing amid this situation, you will keep your eyes on His ability and not your own. Your words are powerful, and they will create an atmosphere. So make sure to speak what God has said and don't talk about the situation. Undoubtedly, one day you will awaken and not remember that it ever happened. If you hold fast to the Lord, you will see the goodness He had planned all along!

Meditation is the key to keeping anxiety out of your life. Paul taught us well in Philippians' book by telling us which things to meditate on during these times.

"Finally, brethren, whatever things are true, whatever things are noble, whatever things are just, whatever things are pure, whatever things are lovely, whatever things are of good report, if there is any virtue and if there is anything praiseworthy; meditate on these things. The things which you learned and received and heard and saw in me, these do, and the God of peace will be with you."

What does it mean to meditate? Keep your mind fixed on Him. The prophet Isaiah shared with us a straightforward way to stay in peace. When you are in peace, you will not be anxious. In Chapter 26, verse 3 of the Book of Isaiah, the Word instructs us to keep our minds stayed on Him, and thereby He will keep us in perfect peace because we trust Him. The Message says it like this, *"People with their minds set on you, you keep completely whole, steady on their feet, because they keep at it and don't quit."*

Another way we can meditate is to keep our hearts full of His promises. We do this by keeping our hearts full of His Word. I love what Psalm 37:3-4 says: *"Trust in the LORD, and do good; Dwell in the land and feed on His faithfulness. Delight yourself also in the LORD, And He shall give you the desires of your heart."* As we meditate on the Word, we feed on His faithfulness.

The Word is your foundation. It is what will stabilize you through the waiting period for the full manifestation of God's promise and provision. The Word is a stabilizing force. When you stand on the Word of God, you are standing on a firm foundation. You will not be toppled over or cast away. Build your house on the foundation. "House" is symbolic of you as the temple of the Holy Spirit. Your body is your house on this earth. You must know and believe that God's Word is true. It is forever settled, so stand firmly upon it. He changes not. He watches over His Word to perform it in my life (Isaiah 55:11).

The word "meditate" is used 11 times in the Psalms.

In Psalm 4:4b, *"to meditate on your bed and be still."* The word "meditate" literally means *to COMMUNE with God*. In the Hebrew, "meditate" also means to: *consider, declare, demand, desire, determine, promise, publish, report, require, say, speak (against, of), talk, and tell.*

So you can see that meditation is not just sitting alone in a quiet room humming. Meditation is active, as well as introspective. It's incredible, too, that meditate here means to *speak, to declare, to demand*. A powerful principle when put into practice that will produce an atmosphere charged with the presence of God.

God is looking for a relationship, a friend, someone who - no matter what happens will turn their heart and mind toward Him, fully trusting Him that everything will turn out okay. If you keep your mind stayed on Him all day, nothing will overtake you. He will become your integral portion, and you will walk in perfect peace in every situation.

Jesus instructed us in Matthew 11:29-30, *"Take My yoke upon you and learn from Me, for I am gentle and lowly in heart, and you will find rest for your souls. For My yoke is easy and My burden is light!* I love how the Message paraphrase puts it, *"Walk with me and work with me, watch how I do it. Learn the unforced rhythms of grace. I won't lay anything heavy or ill-fitting on you. Keep company with me, and you'll learn to live freely and lightly."*

If you want to live a life free from fear and anxiety, you will keep your mind on Him and meditate on all His promises.

Put His words in your mouth and start saying what God has already said. Then He will watch over His Word to perform it in your life, and you will live a carefree life as you allow God to take care of your every need!

Chapter Thirteen

No Fear Lives Here!

"*Perfect love casts out ALL fear...*" 1 John 4:18

The entire verse of 1 John 4:18 says, "*There is no fear in love; but perfect love casts out fear because fear involves torment. But he who fears has not been made perfect in love.*"

If perfect love casts out fear and you are struggling with fear right now, then how can you determine where your love needs to be perfected?

First, look at your love walk toward others. 1 John 4:12 says, "*If we love one another, God abides in us, and His love has been perfected in us.*" And Proverbs 17:17

declares, *"A friend loves at all times..."* Jesus gave each of us a new commandment in John 13:34-35. He said, *"A new commandment I give to you, that you love one another; as I have loved you, that you also love one another..."*

Ask yourself some questions.

1. Am I walking in love toward those around me?
2. How am I responding to those who mistreat me?

Second, test your life by God's definition of love from 1 Corinthians 13. According to that part of Scripture, God's love is NOT...

- Envious, jealous, or boastful
- Vainglorious, conceited, arrogant, or prideful
- Rude or unmannerly
- Does not insist on its own way or right,
- Not self-seeking, touchy, fretful, or resentful
- Does not rejoice at injustice, act unbecomingly, or display itself haughtily.

God's love, AGAPE or unconditional, looks like this…

- Endures long,
- Is patient and kind,
- Takes no account of evil done
- Pays no attention to a suffered wrong
- Rejoices when right and truth prevail
- Bears up under anything
- Is ever ready to believe the best of every person
- Its hopes are fade-less under all circumstances
- It endures everything without weakening
- Never fails, never fades out, or becomes obsolete

One thing is sure; if fear is ruling your life or a particular situation, there's a love issue somewhere to be found. Take time to examine yourself today. Ask the Holy Spirit to reveal any area in your life where love is not yet perfected. Then put on love in that situation and watch God turn the whole thing around!

Pray this: Father perfect Your agape, unconditional love in my heart right now. In Jesus' name I pray. Amen!

Chapter Fourteen

Rhythms of Grace

There is nothing more beautiful than a graceful dance with two people moving together in perfect harmony; fluid motion as they glide across the dance floor. He steps left as she steps right, both in harmonious dance.

God wants us to learn to live our life with Him in beautiful harmony. Jesus instructed us in Matthew 11:29 to take on His yoke and burden because they are light and easy to carry. A modern paraphrase crystallizes what Jesus was really talking about here and learned the unforced rhythms of grace.

Grace means *harmony in motion*. By casting our care on Him and taking up His yoke upon us, we learn to live in harmony with His way of taking care of our every need.

I have come to realize that as we learn to live in grace, we begin to walk in the ebbs and flows of heaven. As we live in God's ways and wholly rely on His help in every area, we truly become partakers of His Divine nature.

Peter said in 2 Peter 1:2—4 that *His divine power has given us all things that pertain to life and godliness.* We received exceedingly great and precious promises. Through these promises of God, when they become a part of our life actively, we become partakers of His character. As these attributes come together, we experience heaven on earth, because we learned to tap into the grace that flows from God.

When heaven is manifest on earth, Psalm 85 illustrates what happens in verses 10 through 13; check out this magnificent list;

- Mercy and truth have met together
- Righteousness and peace have kissed
- Truth shall spring out of the earth
- Righteousness shall look down from heaven
- The LORD will give what is good

- Our land will yield its increase
- Righteousness will go before Him
- Will make His footsteps our pathway

In other words, we must learn to move at the impulse of His Spirit. I often think of verse 13 (His footsteps our pathway!) and remembered when I was a little girl, my dad would let me put my feet on top of his. He would then walk me around as I squealed with delight.

I think of this when verse 13 comes to mind, except it's God's feet, and we are putting our feet on His so that He can walk us down His pathway. It also makes me think of dancing. God moves, I move, He turns, and I turn. It's a fluid motion; He directs my every step as I totally surrender to Him.

Lay down your burdens and cares today. Put your feet on top of His feet and let Him lead the way. Learn the unforced rhythms of grace, the ebbs and flows of heaven. Oh, how wonderful it is when all the power of heaven comes together in perfect harmony with your life.

As you follow Him in this manner, you will experience a life filled with heaven on earth!

Chapter Fifteen

Be it Unto Me

One of the most powerful prayers in the Bible came through Mary, "*Be to me according to Your Word...*" ~ Luke 1:38

There are several examples in Scripture of powerful, sacrificial prayers. When you pray these few simple words, they will change your life in an instant.

Each prayer comes from an individual who dared to give God total control of their life; to bend, make, and mold him or her into what He created them to be. All went on to do marvelous things for God. Today we can glean wisdom and understanding from each.

MARY, MOTHER OF JESUS

Upon hearing the angel's word, Mary prayed one of the most powerful prayers anyone has ever uttered. In Luke 1:38, she responded to the message, "Let it be to me according to Your Word."

Think for a moment; she had just heard the most incredible news - the unfathomable, unexplainable news that she would give birth to the son of God. Right before her declaration, Mary said, "*Behold the maidservant of the Lord.*" In doing so, she established her commitment to God and her heart of humility, reverence, and desire to serve. She was completely willing to let God mold and shape her life for Divine purpose. Even now, I feel like I can hear her thoughts; I am Yours to do with as You please.

Oh, what extraordinary faith and trust in an awesome God! What an incredible sacrifice of all that life was thought to be! Now it's all God's and His for the perfecting and bringing forth of what He chooses.

THE PROPHET ISAIAH

Similar is Isaiah's proclamation in 6:8b, "*Here I am Lord, send me.*"

The Lord just asked a question. "Whom shall I send and who will go for us?" Isaiah being willing and hungry to fulfill the plan of God for his life, boldly answered, "I will go, choose me, send me." At that point, Isaiah had no idea where God was going to send him. In blind faith, he said, "Yes!"

OUR EXAMPLE IN JESUS

Jesus' simple yet powerful prayer in the Garden of Gethsemane. After contending with the Father over the events that were about to unfold? Jesus knew that He was going to pay the ultimate price for the salvation of all humanity. His prayer was so earnest that he began to sweat drops of blood. The Scripture reveals something remarkable. Knowing these things, Jesus lifted His eyes and asked the Father to take the cup from Him, thinking it too hard to bear. But realizing there was no one to stand in His place, He said, "*Nevertheless not my will, but Yours be done*" (Luke 22:42).

Once He prayed this sacrificial prayer, an angel from Heaven appeared, and the Word says the angel strengthened Him, Luke 22:43. The grace or power to endure came to Him after He surrendered, not before. Take note here; there's a lesson!

Jesus gave us another similar prayer as a model in the Sermon on the Mount. He taught us to pray: "*Your* (God's) *kingdom come, Your will be done, on earth as it is in Heaven*" (Matthew 6:10), which takes our hands off the situation and causes us to lift them in solemn surrender to the will of God. It's the best prayer to pray in every situation as you invite God in to do as He wills.

In every situation on earth, you can pray these simple, sacrificial prayers. Why is it so important to give God free reign in your life? 1 Corinthians 13:9 reveals that we know in part and we prophesy in part, which means that your prayers, when in words of understanding, can only be according to what you already know.

God knows the whole picture. He knows it all and has prepared your path for everything you will experience on earth. When you pray as Jesus taught or by the example of other servants of God, you leave the door wide open for God to move on in.

You can settle this right now. God's will is always according to His Word. It will be wonderful and glorious, full of goodness and joy. Desire His will today, and then yield your life to Him by praying these sacrificial prayers. According to His will and according to His Word, there's nothing more powerful!

Pray this: Father, have Your way in me, fulfill all of Your purpose and will through my life. Be it unto to me according to Your Word. In Jesus' name Amen.

Chapter Sixteen

The Key of David

God called David a "man after His own heart." Why? I believe the answer began in the sheepfold when he was just a shepherd boy. He was a musician and a psalmist who was a true worshipper of God.

Worship is not just singing songs to Jesus. Worship is extravagant respect, esteem, honor, and reverence of God. When wrought out in the life of a Christian, it is a lifestyle that will produce great fruit and victory in every area of life. Developing a lifestyle of worship will position you before the throne of God.

Jesus encouraged us to a life of worship. In John 4:23–24, He said to the woman at the well, *"The hour is coming, and now is, when the true worshipers will worship the Father in spirit and truth; for the Father is seeking such to worship Him. God is Spirit, and those who worship Him must worship in spirit and truth."*

When I am ministering, I often look around at the faces of the people during worship. Amazingly, I see so many just standing there with folded arms. I have repeatedly pleaded with the Lord in prayer for them to let down their guard and come into full awareness of God's presence during these powerful times. I so desperately want people to know that He is real and that He wants to show them His goodness.

Like everything else in life, whatever we give our time to will increase; if we give our time each day to worshiping the Lord, then we will experience more of His presence in our life. Let's look at some keys to developing this vital part of our life in God.

CULTIVATE INTENSE LOVE FOR HIM

Do this by remembering what He has done for you. He died for you and paid the price for every sin you would ever commit. All He asks us to do in return is LOVE. The first commandment was to love the Lord our God with all our heart, soul, and strength. In other words, love Him with all that is in you. Give Him all you are. As you cultivate this love for God, you will begin to love others and yourself more intensely.

PURSUE HIM

When you seek Him, you will find Him (Jeremiah 29:13). Pursuing God will take you into a deep relationship with Him. Worship is an easy way to discover God's presence. Your worship attracts Him. He inhabits the praises of His people. Inhabit means *to live in or occupy*. Wow, God lives in your worship. He will occupy your worship. Just think, the more you worship God, the more of Him you will have in your life. Pursue Him in worship!

EFFECTS OF WORSHIP

- Bring You into a Closer Relationship with God

- Lifts Your Spirit
- A Battle Cry Preceding Victory

First, Paul was a true worshiper in every sense of the word. He got it! He found the answer that will lead everyone into a closer relationship with God. He said the most powerful words that have ever impacted my life in Philippians 3:9 & 10. I'm going to paraphrase right from my heart here: For it is MY determined purpose that I may know Him, that I may become progressively more intimately acquainted with Him, perceiving and recognizing His person. Intimately knowing God happens in a life of continual communion with Him; a life given to worship.

We should all cry out to God in times of trouble. God answers the cries of His people. Worship itself is a battle cry preceding victory. In 2 Chronicles 20:15-22, we see King Jehoshaphat in a dilemma where the armies of many enemies were coming out against Israel to drive the people out of their land. The Word of the Lord came to them, saying, "do not be afraid. You will not have to fight in this battle," a comforting thought to know that God had already taken care of it. A revelation that will cause you to worship the Lord and thank Him for what He has done.

The Lord instructed the people to go out against the army, position themselves, stand still, and see the deliverance of the Lord. When the word came, the people began to worship the Lord with a booming voice. The next day, as they were going out to stand against the armies, King Jehoshaphat appointed men to go before the army, singing praises of thanksgiving to the Lord. As the worship went up before the throne of God, the enemy armies turned against one another and defeated themselves.

Worship will also lift your spirit. Isaiah 61:3 tells us to put on the garment of praise for the spirit of heaviness. When you lift your voice to God, thanking Him and worshiping Him despite your circumstance, God will give you the victory. He will lift the heaviness, the burden, the distress, the depression right off of you and replace it with peace and a quiet assurance that all is well.

The key to David's life was worship. He knew how to get right to the heart of God. Worship! Worship is a beautiful way to practice the presence of God. Psalm 100:4 tells us exactly how to get into the presence of God. It tells us how to enter into the heavenly habitation. Enter His gates with thanksgiving and enter His courts with praise. Following the Psalmist's instruction gets you right into the center of God's presence.

Set some time aside every day to worship the Lord and sit in His presence. Then stay connected to Him in your heart. I love what Ephesians 5:19 & 20a says, "Speak to one another with psalms, hymns, and spiritual songs. Sing and make music in your heart to the Lord, always giving thanks to God the Father for everything…"

Then you will be like King David, a man/woman after God's own heart, a true worshipper!

Chapter Seventeen

Living Selflessly

Many years ago, I heard someone say, "until we die to self, we are never going to come into the fullness of what God has for us," which took me straight to the altar of my heart. I began to cry out to God, asking Him to remove everything that would separate me from Him, and prevent His plan from coming to pass in my life.

Do you know that when we ask God to do something that lines up with His will, we can be assured He will bring it to pass? As I asked God to remove the things that kept me separated from Him, He began to reveal those things to me and help me deal with each one. He changed and rearranged my heart, which felt to me like everything in my life.

Real change requires a heart change. And, as you know, any kind of change in our lives can be very uncomfortable.

However, change is an integral part of our walk with God. He is progressively transforming us into the image of His dear Son. So change, whether we have asked for it or coming as a part of our walk with God, is inevitable.

When change comes, sometimes we think the devil is attacking us. However, this is not always the case. Many times, God is trying to make that change in us, which will propel us into the next level of our calling. I heard Joyce Meyer once say, "Our enemies are not our problem because our God is bigger than any of them. Our problem is ourselves and our willingness to submit to God."

If we do not yield to what God is trying to do, we can miss that part of the call on our life. Are you willing and obedient? If you are, you will begin to lay down the things God is revealing to you. The Word says in Isaiah 1:19, "if you are willing and obedient, you will eat the good of the land." And in John 14:15, Jesus said, *"If you love me you will keep my commandments* (obey me)."

Does that mean you will never have to deal with these issues again? No! It means that you have a revelation of who

God is and what He wants you to do. And, because God has told you to do something, you have purposed in your heart to do it without question. By doing this, you tell God that what He wants matters more than anything else in your life (this is the fear of the Lord). And regardless of how you feel, you are determined to follow Him and His way of doing and being right (this is the kingdom of God).

As we walk with God, He is continually teaching and encouraging us to submit ourselves to Him and others. When we begin to do this, we are taking the first steps of dying to ourselves. How can we identify the meaning of "dying to self"? Put other's needs above our own. Follow God's Word regardless of what our flesh wants to do. Do things the way our husbands and employers ask us to do, even though we think it could be done better in a different way. Love others unconditionally, regardless of the pain and hurt they might have caused.

As we do these things, we learn to rely on and trust God more and more, thereby allowing our own needs, wants, and desire to be sacrificed on the altar. And, ultimately, this is required of us as we die to self: Trusting God to meet our own needs as we meet the needs of others; trusting God that He will reward those who obey His commandments; giving our hurt and pain to God, trusting Him to replace it with joy and peace.

If you are in a difficult situation with someone and feel unable to heal from the pain, ask God to give you His heart for that person. I believe that this is one of the greatest gifts of God. His heart for each of us is filled with mercy and compassion regardless of our mistakes. When we have His heart for the person who hurt us, there is no more pain in us, only love for that person - unconditional love flowing through us from the Father. When we don't confess the hurt and pain, it holds us captive in our heart, preventing healing. Admitting it or giving it to God allows Him the ability to take it from us and replace it with the joy He wants to give.

The bottom line is, we must learn to trust God. Dying to self puts us in a place of total dependency on Him, enabling the abundant fruit of our lives to spring forth. As we submit ourselves to Him in deeper ways, His will, plan, and purpose unfold for our life.

It is evident in His word that to bear fruit, we must first die to self. Jesus said in John 12:24, *"I assure you, most solemnly I tell you, unless a grain of wheat falls into the earth and dies, it remains [just one grain; it never becomes more, but lives] by itself alone. But if it dies, it produces many others and yields a rich harvest."*

Our first death is found in the new birth when we receive Jesus as Lord and Savior. When we give our lives to Jesus, we decide to follow Him, and following Him requires specific changes in our lives. As we change the way we view and do things, the "old man" is gone, and the new man or woman springs forth.

2 Corinthians 5:17 says, *"Therefore, if anyone is in Christ, he is a new creation; old things have passed away; behold, all things have become new."* However, our death is not finished there. We continually die to different facets of ourselves as we walk with God and purpose to follow Him, desiring to obey His way of doing things. His way of doing

and being right is found throughout the Scripture. Depending on our sensitivity to the Holy Spirit and our newfound understanding of God's ways, we may next die to lust for cigarettes, beer, alcohol, or food.

Maybe we will overcome the problem of dealing with anger or jealousy. Sometimes this first battle can be long, but as we purpose in our hearts to follow God, we are assured victory. *"For whatever is born of God overcomes the world. And this is the victory that has overcome the world, even our faith. Who is he who overcomes the world, but he who believes that Jesus is the Son of God?"* (1 John 5:4, 5). Each step, each day, propels us closer to overcoming the weight of sin that so easily holds us back. Jesus said, *"Be of good cheer for I have overcome the world"* (John 16:33).

I recently heard an evangelist say that if you get knocked down seven times, get up eight! Never give up. Refuse to fail. The Word says in Matthew 19:26, *"with God all things are possible."* It's incredible how knowing and walking with God is such a tremendous process, a process of new levels and greater opportunities. If we are truly following God, our ascent will be upward to the call of God (Philippians 3:14). However, if we are descending or standing still, we can be sure that there is an area in our life to be dealt with, and we may even know what it is! If we are not sure of what it is, we can ask God to reveal it, and He will. He will by no means withhold any good thing from those who walk uprightly (Psalm 84:11).

And we can be sure that the Holy Spirit will not temp and taunt us by not revealing the next step. He has been dealing with us the whole time. Either we don't want to hear what He is saying, or we are blinded by deception and can't see it. We are deceived when we focus our eyes on someone or something other than God. Often when God is trying to deal with us concerning something He wants to remove from our heart, we think God is talking about someone else. God will not consult us about what someone else is or is not doing. Jesus said in Matthew 7:3, 5, *"And why beholdest thou the mote that is in thy brother's eye, but considerest not the beam that is in thine own eye? Hypocrite, first cast out the beam out of thine own eye, and then shalt thou see clearly to cast out the mote out of thy brother's eye."* Now there may be occasions in prayer when God puts a burden on our heart about someone else so that we can pray for that person. But when dealing with us openly, He does not reveal things to us about others. We are the ones being dealt with when revelation comes! *"Therefore, let him who thinks he stands take heed lest he fall"* (1 Corinthians 10:12). By revealing things, God is trying to get us to recognize our sinful nature and, by doing so, bring us to repentance, causing us to yield ourselves to Him so that by His Spirit, the sin can be removed from us. We would save ourselves a lot of heartaches if we would just lay ourselves on the altar and let God have His way in our lives. I'm not talking about selling all your possessions; I'm talking about a change of heart that affects your life, such as how people begin to see more of Jesus in you.

1 John 3:16 (AMP) says, *"By this, we come to know (progressively to recognize, to perceive, to understand) the [essential] love: that He laid down His own life for us; and we ought to lay [our] lives down for [those who are our]*

brothers [in Him]." Jesus said in John 15:13 (AMP), *"No one has greater love [no one has shown stronger affection] than to lay down (give up) his own life for his friends."*

If we are to go on with the things of God, we must forsake ourselves and seek Him. Set your mind on things above, not on things on the earth (Colossians 3:2). Setting your mind on the things above is simply setting your mind on the Lord and seeking to do His will by serving Him. How do we serve God on this earth? By serving others, we are His arms and hands in the earth. With the Holy Spirit, we can touch others' lives for the Kingdom and change them forever, giving God all the glory for His inner working in us.

We stop looking for what we will get from God and look for what we can give to God. The Word says in Philippians 4:19, "And my God shall supply all your need according to His riches in glory by Christ Jesus." I am convinced that as we go about meeting others' needs, He will abundantly meet our needs when we least expect it. So go ahead, let go of all your desires and needs, give them to God. Take up the cause of other people and help them realize their desires and obtain their needs. Die to self and live for others; this is where God's greatest blessings will be realized in all our lives.

Pray this: Father, I surrender and give my all to you. Take hold of my life and help me completely give myself to you and others in Jesus' name, Amen.

Chapter Eighteen

Hope of Glory

It is no longer I who live, but Christ lives in me. This life I live now in the flesh, I live by faith in Jesus Christ.

It is no longer I who live; I have died; I cease to exist as I did before. What I have - all of it - I have given to Christ for His possession. It is His holy possession to do with as He wills. I offer my body as a living sacrifice, holy and acceptable to God, which is my reasonable service.

Reasonable service? What does that mean? It is my service to God, my total reliance upon Him. Sacrificing my will and desires is my complete surrender to Him that requires all of me – spirit, soul, and body. It is my reasonable service; my fair service; my appropriate service; my gift back to Him for giving His life for me. Dying to selfish desires is my spiritual act of worship and an offering that He will accept.

To further lay our bodies down, and allow our own lives to be consumed by His, will bring this death. It is no longer I who live, but Christ.

Have you ever asked yourself what will happen to bring us to this place of death? Will a spiritual death cause the death of dreams, the death of relationships, or the loss of possessions? This death is a stripping away of everything thought to be right and true, removing the covering; a deprivation of what was right, but now is no more.

In this season of death, God is saying out with the old and in with the new. God is removing all of that which is familiar. When we try to locate those lost places, we realize they do not exist anymore. There is nothing there; it has passed away, never to be found again. It is dead and gone. He is - and has been - taking us through this death experience to strip away all that is familiar. To purge and empty us, cleanse us, and prepare us for purification.

David had it so right and true in Psalm 51 when he cried out to the Lord and said, "Have mercy upon me ... wash me ... cleanse me ... purge me ... make me hear ...create in me a clean heart ... renew a steadfast spirit within me ... do not cast me away ... do not take Your Holy Spirit from me ... restore me ... uphold me ... deliver me ..."

The sacrifices of God are a broken spirit; and a broken and contrite heart. These, O God, You will not despise.

So are we surprised to be in a place of brokenness, a place of desperation, feeling as though God has left us alone in this battle? We feel as though God has removed His hand and taken His spirit from us. We are in a place of crying out in the spirit, seeking and searching for that which was lost.

We want God to restore all that we have lost, but we have lost what we have lost for Him. We keep looking back at what we have lost, but there's nothing back there. It is dead and gone. When God restores it, it does not look like it did before, and there's no hint of the past. It does not even look like what we expected. As we keep looking back, mourning for that old way, we take our eyes off Jesus. God is saying, turn around and look ahead. That's what restoration means in Hebrew and Greek: *turn around, turn away from that which is of old.* Look forward, look straight on to the new way, the new life, the perfect way of the Lord.

When you give God all of you, He begins to restore, renew, and bring you into a great blessing.

Job was tested, and the Word says Job was a righteous man. God revealed His awesomeness to Job, and Job repented in dust and ashes, realizing he never really knew God. As I mentioned earlier in this book, Jesus was tested. The Spirit Himself led Jesus away into the wilderness to be tested for 40 days. Upon completing this season of suffering, the Word says that Jesus came out in the POWER of the SPIRIT. If He was tested, then you will be tested. But know that this testing of your faith will work out for your good.

1 Peter 1:6-7 reveals something fantastic. It says, *"though now for a little while you may have had to suffer grief in all kinds of trials. These have come so that your faith - of greater worth than gold, which perishes even though refined by fire, may be proved genuine and may*

result in praise, glory, and honor when Jesus Christ is revealed." (NIV)

Notice the Scripture says that our suffering in trials is proving our faith genuine. And further, the clause in the middle of the sentence reveals our faith is of more excellent value than gold that perishes, even though it is refined with fire. This statement reveals that our faith, when refined with fire, will never cease but live on throughout eternity. Peter went on to tell us, "don't be surprised, rejoice!"

How will we ever be what God has destined us for if we are not demonstrating the nature of God to a dying world? We must be tested and proved. We need to be purified as we overcome adversity to show His love and goodness in the earth.

Peter continues to speak to us in 4:19, saying, *"So then, those who suffer according to God's will should commit themselves to their faithful Creator and continue to do good."* (NIV)

We must persevere and continue to serve with faithfulness. But God is not telling us to serve in quietness before Him. The Scripture tells us to lift our voice to Him. We are to lament and to cry out His name. When He hears us, He will deliver us out of our suffering.

Why are our tears so important? Tears are liquid prayer. When we cry, our tears are seed, and our tears sow seed into our future. Every tear will bring a harvest. Tears conceive and bring forth and give birth to God's plans. Tears move the hand of God. They get the attention of the Lord, turning His favor toward the one weeping.

During these times of mourning, God requires us to rend our hearts and not our garments. In the old days, the lamenters, the mourners, ripped their clothes and sat weeping in sackcloth and ashes, which is not what God seeks. He's looking for the rending, the tearing to pieces, the piercing, and the tremendous emotional pain experienced in a broken heart.

Perhaps your tears have been your food day and night (Ps. 42:3). Maybe you have been annihilated, beaten down, abused, mistreated, and so destroyed that you thought you could not bear to go on. The mercy and love of God are here to renew, renovate and restore.

The Lord says to you today; He has heard your cries. They have come up before His throne, and He hears. Everything is about to change for you. You have been emptied, stripped of everything familiar, and God is saying today, "Behold I will do a new thing in you, and the whole world will watch in amazement, saying indeed the Lord their God is with them. Many will tremble, even in the church, expressing God's greatness has been shown forth, and in this, we are glad. Great rejoicing will be heard from Zion as His presence refreshes his church.

Perhaps, because of your harshness of heart, you have not shed the first tear. You are angry, rebellious, caught up in sin, refusing to turn, refusing to forgive, and demanding justice from a harsh world that does not seem to care if you live or die. People laugh in your face and scorn you. Because you won't cry out to God, you have chosen the desert, the parched ground, to serve the taskmaster. Today, your deliverance is near you. Thus, says the Lord, I will melt your heart and try you that you will be mine.

The prophet Joel told us in chapter 2, verses 12 &13, *"even now,' declares the LORD, 'return to me with all your heart, with fasting and weeping and mourning.' Rend your heart and not your garments. Return to the LORD your God, for he is gracious and compassionate, slow to anger and abounding in love, and he relents from sending calamity."* (NIV)

Notice what is said, "Return and He will relent." He will remove and release you from the burden, but you must return.

Job 11:13-19, *"Yet if you devote your heart to him and stretch out your hands to him if you put away the sin that is in your hand and allow no evil to dwell in your tent, then you will lift your face without shame; you will stand firm and without fear. You will surely forget your trouble, recalling it only as waters gone by. Life will be brighter than noonday, and darkness will become like morning. You will be secure, because there is hope; you will look about* you and take your rest in safety. You will lie down, with no one to make you afraid, and many will court your favor." (NIV)

Jeremiah 9:17-19 tells us it's essential to have weeping that there is no one to weep and call in the professionals! The Scripture says here, *"This is what the LORD Almighty says: 'Consider now, Call for the wailing women to come; send for the most skillful of them. Let them come quickly and wail over us till our eyes overflow with tears, and water streams from our eyelids. The sound of wailing is heard from Zion:"* (NIV)

Why did God tell Jeremiah to call for the most skillful wailing women? By their skill in weeping and mourning, these women invoked others to weep with passion and intensity. They wept until every eye around them was full of tears. Why did Jeremiah have to call for the professional weepers? Our answers lie in Jeremiah 3:1-19. The people's hearts were hardened, and they needed restoration and healing.

Why do we need restoration? Because we have fallen away from God! Here the Scripture tells us several things that happened. People were not valiant for the truth. They have become complacent and bitter, hard-hearted speaking lies and deceit. Many have adjoined themselves to wrong things, and no one can trust another. Then God says an amazing thing, He says, *"How else can I deal with my daughter than to refine and try her?"* (verse7). God's judgment is coming to bring us back to Him so that He can restore us. It is His mercy in operation to reveal the hidden things of our hearts. Judgment will bring death to those who don't respond, and grace, peace, and joy to those who do. When God announces His judgment, the people lament and mourn. Their lamentation and mourning is the very thing that moves the hand of God and causes Him to relent and bring them back into full fellowship with Him. Therefore, our hearts must be broken. We must weep, as in Joel's day, between the porch and the altar of God.

Acts 3:19 tells us that we must repent and turn so that times of refreshing will come in the presence of the Lord. If we continue in our sinful ways with no sorrow in our hearts, we will be separated from the presence of the Lord. When we turn around, refreshing comes. Refreshing means recovery and revival.

Remember Job, the righteous man. He lost everything. His friends tried to help, but they only led him the wrong way. Have you tried to reach out to those around you for help, but they didn't understand? They only commiserated with you. They didn't give you the information you needed to get out of your situation. They just helped you to stay there.

That's what happened to Job. Then a wise young man showed up and told Job about the awesomeness of God. As Elihu declared who God was to Job, then an amazing thing happened. God, Himself showed up. When God showed up and began to show Himself to Job, Job realized he only knew God peripherally, in his head. But now Job's heart was awakened. His heart had been pierced and broken to pieces as he realized he had only heard by the hearing of his ear, but now he sees with spiritual eyes. At this moment, in the presence of God, Job repented and turned. Then God began the process of restoration. The Word says that in the end, God blessed Job more than at the beginning. The Scripture says that Job received double of what he had in the beginning.

There is a process to restoration, and we see it patterned repeatedly in the Scripture. If something needs to be restored, then it has grown old and decayed. It has lost something that it once had. We need to be brought back into an intimate relationship with God. We must turn around. We must return.

The process of doing this is first to acknowledge where you are. Take ownership of your life and responsibility for where you are. Admit the truth and admit the existence of sin. Then repent, and I mean true repentance with godly sorrow. Do you not know that you have trampled the Blood of Jesus underfoot by even partaking of such things? You have grieved the Holy Spirit by taking Him into places that you would not take your mother. If you would not take your mother or grandmother there, then why do you take your

Savior? Repent with weeping, repent with mourning and forgive those who have used and abused you. Forgive and let go. Forgive and walk free. Then - and only then - will this Scripture ring right for you. Psalm 126;

When the LORD restored his exiles to Jerusalem,
it was like a dream! We were filled with laughter,
and we sang for joy.
And the other nations said, what amazing things the LORD has done for them! Yes, the LORD has done amazing things for us! What joy!
Restore our fortunes, LORD, as streams renew the desert. Those who plant in tears will harvest with shouts of joy. They weep as they go to plant their seed, but they sing as they return with the harvest. (NLT)

Lay it all down, let it go. Relinquish, give it up, and take up the life of Christ. Declare boldly, "It is no longer I who live but Christ lives in me!"

Chapter Nineteen

High Calling

We should be continually growing in God, in revelation, understanding, and friendship. As we purpose in our hearts to follow God, walk with Him, and endeavor to be like Him, we will grow in grace. When Jesus was just a boy, the Scripture says of Him in Luke 2:40, "And the Child grew and became strong in spirit, filled with wisdom; and the grace of God was upon Him." Just as He grew and became strong in spirit and filled with wisdom, so are we as we walk with God. Literally, the phrase "the grace of God was upon Him" means that God's divine influence upon the heart and the reflection of it was demonstrated in His life.

And, of course, as Jesus grew, in developed and demonstrated more and more of the divine influence of God in His life, which is God's desire for us as well. When we give ourselves to this, we ascend into God—ascending means to rise in status, climb or go up. Another meaning of the word "ascend" is *to grow or increase*. It is God's plan for our lives that we are ever-growing and ever-increasing in Him.

Enoch's life is a powerful demonstration of ascension. It is said of Enoch in Genesis 5 that he walked with God. A phrase mentioned not once but twice, in verses 22 & 24. Then the Scripture abruptly says that Enoch was not for God took him. Over the years, Enoch has become such a champion to me of those who knew their God. I wonder what his life was like for the writer to mention in the middle of a genealogy that Enoch walked with God? We know from Scripture that two cannot walk together unless they are agreed. We know from Paul's teachings in the book of Hebrews that Enoch pleased God, and that's why God took him. Enoch did not see death. God translated or raptured him right out of here! Enoch must have been a friend and compatriot of God. He had given his life to the Lord's service and never wavered. Throughout his life, Enoch was continually growing, increasing, and rising in status with

God. He became so full of God that the earth could not contain him anymore. I believe this is the future of the body of Christ. When the church is snatched out of here at the rapture, we will be so full of God that the earth cannot hold us. A state of living wrought out progressively, we walk with God and embracing His ways. We are ever ascending into Him.

Isaiah 35:8 speaks of a road called the Highway of Holiness. This road is the road that takes us higher into God. Everyone who is born again is on the road. The Scripture says that even if you are a fool, you won't ere in the way if you stay on the Highway. Now we can look at this highway from several different perspectives. First is the obvious, a road that leads up into heaven. As we live our lives in God, we grow in the knowledge of Him and continually go from faith to faith and glory to glory growing and going higher and higher up the road into heaven. Another way to look at this road is to think of living a "high *way*" of life. Living life with high standards, holy, sanctified, and set apart for God's plans and purposes only. Either way, as we seek to do the things God has taught us through His Word, we will grow and increase in Him.

As we do so, we will become full of His divine influence, and the reflection of it will be demonstrated through us, just as it was through Jesus.

Chapter Twenty

Declare Him

Job 22:28 says, "*Declare a thing, and it shall be established, so that light will shine on your ways.*"

I want to share what happens on the inside of you when you declare, with your mouth, the works of the Lord. Let's look more closely at the Scripture leading up to Job 22:28.

Starting in verse 21, the Word says, "*Now acquaint yourself with Him, and be at peace; Thereby good will come to you. Receive, please, instruction from His mouth, and lay up His words in your heart. If you return to the Almighty, you will be built up; you will remove iniquity far from your tents. Then you will lay your gold in the dust, and the gold of Ophir among the stones of the brooks. Yes, the Almighty will be your gold and your precious silver; For then you will have your delight in the Almighty, and lift up your face to God. You will make your prayer to Him, He will hear you, and you will pay your vows. You will also declare a thing, and it will be established for you; so light will shine on your ways. When they cast you down, and you say, 'Exaltation will come!' Then He will save the humble person. He will even deliver one who is not innocent; yes, he will be delivered by the purity of your hands."*

For every promise of God, there are some caveats. I want to look at several words throughout this Scripture to fully understand what God is saying as He leads up to verse 28. "Acquaint" means *to know Him*. The phrase "lay-up" means *to rehearse, mark, consider, putting on, or holding onto His words in your heart*. "Built-up" means *to be repaired and made into the person He has created you to be*. In the phrase, "you will delight in Him;" the word "delight" means *to be soft and pliable toward His promptings*. In other words, when you do these things: Know Him, lay up His words in your heart, made into the person He has created you to be, and remain soft and pliable toward His prompting, then you will declare a thing, and it will be established. What do we declare? We declare who He is, what He has done, and what He is about to do! We declare His Word.

From the very beginning, God's people have been declaring His works. The Word says of Joshua that he made known all the works of the Lord. Nehemiah said to the people, *"Do not be afraid of your enemies, remember the Lord, great and awesome."* David was always remembering and declaring the works of the Lord. In Psalm 77:11, he said, *"Remember the works of the Lord."* And, in Psalm 105:5, *"Remember His marvelous works."* Solomon said to remember His great love in Song of Solomon. Micah noted in chapter 6, verse 5, *"Remember that you may know the righteousness of the Lord"* (6:5). And Habakkuk declared, *"In wrath remember mercy"* (3:2).

Perhaps one of the great demonstrations of what happens when we declare the works of the Lord can be read in the book of Job. Job had been through a lot. He was a servant of God but had lost everything he had, children and livelihood. His friends tried to console him, but what they were doing was commiserating with him about all his woes and why they happened-none of which were the answer Job needed from God. A young man named Elihu came on the scene in Chapter 32 and began to speak. First, he contradicts Job's friends and then contradicts Job with God's truth concerning his circumstances. Then Elihu does an amazing thing; he begins to declare God, Himself. He begins to declare the works of the Lord. He proclaims God's justice, God's goodness, and God's majesty.

What happens next? God shows up! The manifest presence of almighty God! Think about the significance of God manifesting His presence where His marvelous and glorious works are declared. What an amazing thing, where God is declared, He shows up!

Let's look at another amazing fact. Throughout the Old Testament, The Ark of the Covenant was the only place where God's presence dwelt. The ark contained three things: The Ten Commandments, Aaron's Rod, and a pot of Manna; symbols of God's Word, God's power and authority, and God's glory and provision. All three things were symbols of who God is and what He has done. Think of the significance of this, His presence dwells in a place where He is remembered and declared. God dwells where He is the focus, where He is remembered, and where He is declared. He wants to be commemorated in our lives by word and deed through showing respect and affection for all He has done.

In the days of old, God's glory dwelt in the temple at the Ark of the Covenant, but today He dwells in His people. How do you allow the presence and power of God to manifest in your life? Set His works; His goodness, righteousness, glory, majesty, covenant, etc.

David wrote a tribute to God when the Ark of the Covenant was returned to the temple. He wrote;

Sing to the Lord, all the earth, proclaim the good news of His salvation from day to day, declare His glory among the nations, His wonders among all peoples.

Give to the Lord the glory due His name, bring an offering and come before Him. Oh, worship the Lord in the beauty of holiness.

Oh, give thanks to the Lord for He is good! His mercy endures forever. And say, save us, O God of our salvation, gather us together and deliver us to give thanks to Your holy name and to triumph in Your praise.

Do you need God to show up in some area of your life? Maybe even every area of your life! The bottom line in all of this is to start declaring the works of the Lord. It is easy to declare what we know from the Scriptures, and we should do so, but what has He done in your life? Those works you must commemorate and declare. Did He save you? Did He bring you out of devastation? Has He preserved your life? Is your name written in the Lamb's Book of Life? Psalm 63 gives us good instruction and powerful things to remember:

O God you are my God; I earnestly search for You. My soul thirsts for You, my whole body longs for You in this parched and weary land where there is no water. I have seen you in your sanctuary and gazed upon Your power and glory. Your unfailing love is better to me than life itself, how I praise You! I will honor you as long as I live, lifting up my hands to You in prayer. You satisfy me more than the richest of foods. I will praise You with songs of Joy. I lie awake thinking of You, meditating on You through the night. I think how much You have helped me; I sing for joy in the shadow of Your protecting wings. I follow close behind You; Your strong right arm holds me securely. (NLT)

Take time to write a tribute to God, commemorating Him for all He has done in your life. Then daily declare it to Him, as you do this, you will see glorious, extraordinary change come into every area of your life.

Epilogue

Answer the One Who Calls!

If you could touch of what I have tasted,

He who fills to all in all,

fullness of joy, inexpressible joy

See with the eyes of Jesus;

hear with His ears, love with His heart

He is calling you, come to Him,

don't deny yourself

The pleasure of knowing the fullness of Him who calls

Come, drink of the river of life

A river flowing with the

awesome and mighty power of God,

Yet overtaking us with gentle waves of tender mercies.

Yield yourself so that His awesome light may

pierce your mortal flesh allowing you to

soar with Him on the wings of eagles far above

the circumstances of this world.

Be clothed with the Father's love,

wrapped tightly into His cleft,

Long to be where He will fill you with His love

Flowing like a rushing river,

overtaking you with His goodness

Clothe us in glory; transform us into the image of our King,

Conform us to His will that we may see

His desire prevail upon us

Time and time again I come,

I come boldly seeking, searching, longing,

looking for my King

I hear Him calling and calling again...

I must answer; I must go to my King.

~ by Charlana Kelly, © 2006

Acknowledgements

To Chuck, I am eternally grateful. You are continually used by God to mold and shape my heart. God sent you in my life. There's no telling where I would be today if not for you! Mere words cannot express my love for you!

To my mother, you are my greatest cheerleader. Thank you for imitating your mom by reading the Bible to me daily as a child and for always telling me that I had it within me to do great things.

To every person who took the time to sow into my life, I am eternal fruit accounted to you! Many of you believed in me before I could believe in myself! You prayed for me, spoke life into my heart, and never turned away. You have been steadfast; because of your faithfulness, I am the woman I am today!

To my prayer partners, Barbara Michael and Michelle Baker, what we share is rare, very rare, but hearts united in the single cause of Christ will NEVER be broken.

And, most of all, to my King! I am eternally grateful to have a King who dreamed of me before I ever longed for Him. He sought me until I yielded my life to Him and turned me right side up so that I could serve Him. Jesus, You are my King!

Jesus, Your throne is God's throne, ever and always; the scepter of your royal rule measures right living. And, that is why God, your very own God, poured fragrant oil on your head, marking you out as king from among your dear companions. Your ozone-drenched garments are fragrant with mountain breeze. Chamber music from the throne room makes you want to dance. Kings' daughters are maids in your court, the Bride glittering with gold jewelry. Now listen daughter, don't miss a word. Forget your country; put your home behind you. Be there the king is wild for you.

Since he's your lord, adore him. Wedding gifts pour in... guests shower you with presents... She is led to the king... A procession of joy and laughter! A grand entrance to the king's palace! (Psalm 45:6-17, MSG)

God says, You are the ones chosen by Him, chosen for the high calling... God's instruments to do his work and speak out for him, to tell others of the night and day difference he made for you B from nothing to something, from rejected to accepted." (1 Peter 2:9-10, MSG)

Glory to God forever!

About the Author

Multiple times author, tv/radio host, Charlana Kelly is passionate about Jesus and people. Her heart's desire is to reach the world with the Good News that they have a Savior in Christ.

You can watch her television program, Engage for Influence, on Grace TV and listen to her weekly radio show, Unshakable, on 104.3 Joy FM East Texas or watch/listen to both on all streaming platforms.

Charlana has been in full-time ministry since 1998, was ordained in 2002, leads international women's ministry through the local church and her Women of Influence Network.

She and her husband of 34 years, Chuck, live in Crockett, TX where they enjoy life and exploring old historic cities. You can connect with her on the social media platforms Facebook, Instagram, and YouTube.

www.ingramcontent.com/pod-product-compliance
Lightning Source LLC
Chambersburg PA
CBHW070911080526
44589CB00013B/1253